Some wild animals make new homes in to
cities. They find safe places amongst all the people.

Herring gull chicks

Mallard duck

Town homes

Buildings

There are often big buildings near the centre of towns. They are like tall cliffs to small animals. Some animals make their homes on these tall buildings. Insects and spiders rest on the walls of the buildings. Birds nest on ledges, or in the spaces under roofs.

Kestrels on ledge of tower block

Swifts nesting

Town animals

CONTENTS

Introduction

Lots of people live and work in towns and cities. As a town grows, woods are cut down and fields are covered in buildings. There is a lot of **pollution**. Most wild animals lose their homes.

Rat feeding on rubbish tip

People throw out food and other things that they do not want. Foxes, mice and rats take food from dustbins and rubbish bags. Animals that do this are called **scavengers**.

Rivers and lakes

Many towns are built beside rivers or big lakes. Fish can live in clean water. Birds nest in the trees that grow by the rivers and lakes.

Parks and gardens

Many towns have parks with rivers and lakes.
Animals find shelter, food and water in parks.
People often visit to feed the birds and squirrels.
People also put food out for birds and hedgehogs
in their gardens.

Town animals

Birds

Pigeons live in almost all towns. Feral pigeons nest on ledges high above the ground. Wood pigeons make nests of twigs in tall trees. Pigeons eat plants. They also eat food given to them by people.

Feral pigeons

Wood pigeons

◀ *Starlings gathering before flying off*

▲
Flocks of starlings circling around before roosting

Most starlings live in the country. Starlings often fly in to towns in the evening. The starlings circle round in huge flocks. Then they **roost** on the big buildings.

Starlings roosting ▶

Swans are the biggest birds that live in towns. They
swim on ponds in the parks. Mallard ducks and
geese and other water birds also swim on the ponds.
In winter, other kinds of ducks sometimes arrive.
These ducks are on their way to find a warm place.

Tawny owl

Birds that hunt other animals live in most towns.
A kestrel is a bird that hunts. It hovers above the
ground, looking for mice or beetles to eat. At night,
tawny owls make a hooting noise as they hunt for
mice or small birds.

Mammals

Grey squirrels are seen in towns more than other wild mammals. They build nests called **dreys** in big, old trees. Squirrels eat all sorts of plants. They also like acorns and nuts.

Squirrel in its drey

Hedgehogs often live in parks and gardens. They hunt
in the evening and at night. They look for worms and
beetles and caterpillars. Hedgehogs have prickles
which protect them from most enemies but not from
cars. Many hedgehogs are killed on the roads in towns.

Mouse gnawing electric cable

Rats and mice live in all towns and cities. They are pests and do a great deal of damage. They eat almost any food. They also harm buildings, by gnawing wood and electric cables.

*Foxes in a
garage*

Foxes live in many towns. They hide in buildings
and other empty places. Sometimes they live beside
railways. Foxes are shy animals. They do not like to
be seen by people. They are mostly **nocturnal**. At
night they come out to hunt for mice and rats, or to
raid dustbins for food.

Wasps' nest on drainpipe

Insects and spiders

In the summer time, insects often rest on the walls of buildings. Little jumping spiders hunt them for food. Wasps make nests on buildings. In the winter, flies called cluster flies sometimes rest in lofts or attics. They do not harm human beings. They fly away when the weather gets warmer.

Butterflies and other insects feed on **nectar**. They find this in the flowers in town parks and gardens. Some people keep hives of bees on the roofs of town buildings. The bees make honey from the nectar that they collect from flowers.

Peacock butterfly on buddleia

Helping town animals

People like to see animals in towns. People can help animals, too. One way to help animals is to make a nature garden.

buddleia

compost bin

pond

new trees

bird table

bird bath

19

Glossary

dreys   Squirrels' nests

nectar   A type of food that bees and other insects find in flowers

nocturnal   An animal that is nocturnal comes out to look for food at night

pollution   Things that spoil the environment, for example, rubbish in streets and dirty water in rivers

roost   When birds roost, they are resting or sleeping

scavengers   Animals that take food left in dustbins and rubbish dumps